Tomekichi Homma: The Story of a Canadian

Tomekichi Homma: The Story of a Canadian

K.T. HOMMA & C.G. ISAKSSON

hancock

house

ISBN-13: 978-0-88839-660-0

Cataloguing in Publication Data

Homma, K. T. (Keiki Tenney-Sean), 1956–
    Tomekichi Homma : the story of a Canadian / K.T. Homma,
    C.G. Isaksson.

    Includes bibliographical references.
    ISBN 978-0-88839-660-0

    1. Homma, Tomekishi, 1865-1945.
    2. Japanese Canadians—British Columbia—Biography.
    3. Japanese—British Columbia—Biography.
    4. Japanese Canadians--Evacuation and relocation, 1942–1945.
    5. Frontier and pioneer life—British Columbia. I. Isaksson, C. G.
    (Carey Georgia), 1950–
    II. Title.

    FC3850.J3Z7 2008   971.1004'9560092   C2008-902523-7

Editor: Theresa Laviolette
Production: Mia Hancock
Cover Design: Mia Hancock
Front cover image: Portrait of Tomekichi Homma (Homma family photo, ca. early 1900s)

*We acknowledge the financial support of the Government of Canada through the
Book Publishing Industry Development Program (BPIDP) for our publishing activities.*

Published simultaneously in Canada and the United States by

HANCOCK HOUSE PUBLISHERS LTD.
19313 Zero Avenue, Surrey, B.C. Canada V3S 9R9
(604) 538-1114 Fax (604) 538-2262

HANCOCK HOUSE PUBLISHERS
1431 Harrison Avenue, Blaine, WA U.S.A. 98230-5005
(604) 538-1114 Fax (604) 538-2262
www.hancockhouse.com
Email: sales@hancockhouse.com

Homma family burial plot in Ichikawa City, Chiba Prefecture. Some of Tomekichi Homma's ashes were taken to Japan and instilled in the family burial site. Generations of Hommas have been cremated and placed there.
(Reverend Miyakawa photo, 1980)

The Family Tree of Tomekichi

本間留吉え家譜

⓪ 本間佐渡守 ‧‧‧‧‧‧‧ 孫太郎
HOMMA SADONOKAMI ‧‧‧‧‧‧‧ 孫太郎

⓪ 太郎兵衛 —— 大坂陣 討死 —— 下而浪人
TAROBEI —— KILLED AT OSAKA BATTLE — RESULT-UNEPLOYED

⓪ 上総久留利城主, 黒田三五郎氏に軍学師範として奉公
SERVED AS MELITARY ADVISER of SANGORO KURODA OWNER of CASTLE
KURURI of KAZUSA

⓪ ジ未旧藩に在り初代小左衛門正治‧‧‧‧其後故あって性と母方の梅沢を名乗
余ノ父小左衛門正定に至り復籍 本間を名乗る.
FROM THERE ON SERVED SAME FEUDAL CLAN BUT LATER ON WITH SOM
UNEXPLAINABLE REASON CHANGED HIS SURNAME TO MOTHERSIDE UMEZA
BUT MY FATHERS TIME KOZAEMON MASATADA'S SURNAME HOMMA RESTOR

● 母は旧藩芝山次エ門ノ妹千代 — 大吉(早世) 口忠吉(新井へ養子) 正理
(土岐へ養子) 正和(継世) 留吉(カナダ)
MY MOTHER WAS FROM OLD FEUDAL CLAN ‧‧‧JIEMON SHIBAYAMA'S SIST
CHIYO, DAIKICHI (PASSED AWAY EARLY) TADAYOSHI (ADOPTED TO ARAI)
MASASATO (ADOPTED TO DOKI) MASAKAZU RESUMED HOMMA, TOMEKICHI
(CANADA)

⓪ 日本の墓地の記憶は上総久留思真勝寺
I REMEMBER CEMETARY IN JAPAN IS SHINSHOJI KURURI KAZUSA

⓪ 東京上野 ナガ上州 沼田
TOKYO UYENO NAGA KAMISU ? NUMADA

⓪ 余ノ実兄正和は下総東葛飾郡 鬼越村 長崎屋惣七ノ娘タマ女と
結婚しキク女 と準一郎 其他を生む.
MY OLDER BROTHER MASAKAZU of SHINOFUSA HIGASHI KATSUSHIKA‧GORI
ONIGOSHI (OR ONIGOE) MURA MARRIED TO NAGASAKIYA SOSHICHI'S DAUGHTER
TAMAE RAISED KIKUME AND JUNICHIRO AND OTHERS.

● 本間留吉 数十年前渡加, 拾年前に死亡. 妻マツ三年前死亡.
TOMEKICHI HOMMA CAME TO CANADA MANY YEARS AGO
HIS WIFE MATSU PASSED AWAY 3 YEARS AGO

6

The writing of Tomekichi Homma.
(Translated by Yoshimaru Abe, date unknown)

足利義氏の家臣 本间佐渡守 源宗正は初代なるも二代より八代まで不明.

HOMMA SADONOKAMI GENJI MUNEMASA IS A 1st. RETAINER OF MASTER
ASHIKAGA YOSHIUJI (FAMILY OF SHOGUN YEAR AROUND 1400)
HOMMA SADONOKAMI GENJI MUNEMASA IS A 1st. RETAINER HOWEVER
2ND. TO 8TH. GENERATIONS ARE NOT KNOWN

九代　　源　正路　　　黒田家臣
9 TH.　GENJI　MASAMICHI　RETAINER OF DAIMYO (WARLORD) KURODA

十代　　本间権右衛門正国　黒田家臣
10 TH.　HOMMA GONUEMON MASAKIJNI RETAINER OF DAIMYO　KURODA

十一代　本间平石衛門 源正永　黒田家臣
11 TH.　HOMMA HEIUEMON GENJI MASANAGA　RETAINER OF DAIMYO KURODA

十二代　本间小左衛門 源 正忠·　正永実子
12 TH.　HOMMA KOZAEMON GENJI MASATADA　SON OF MASANAGA

十三代　本间正利　　　正忠長男
13 TH.　HOMMA MASATOSHI　1ST. SON OF MASATADA

十四代　本间與吉　源正與　正忠三男正利実弟
14 TH　HOMMA YOKICHI GENJI MASAOKI 3RD. SON OF MASATADA (BROTHER OF MASATOSHI)

十五代　本间正　　　正忠四男
15 TH.　HOMMA　　　4 TH SON OF MASATADA

本间留吉　　　1883年 クナダ に渡る
HOMMA TOMEKICHI　EMIGRATED TO CANADA IN 1883
1865 - 1945

妻　マツ
WIFE　MATSU　1880 - 1951

長女　靜枝
1 ST. DAUGHTER　SHIZUE　1902 - 1903

長男　襄　　　　WIFE HASUE 蓮枝 1912-2007
1 ST. SON　JOE　1905- 1968

2ND. SON　JUNKICHI 順吉　1908- 1915

3RD. SON　SEIJI 清次　1911-1964 WIFE SHIZUE 靜江 1915-1990

4 TH. SON　SHINGO 慎吾　1915-1993 " CHIZUE チズエ 1920-1978

5 TH. SON　KEAY 敬　1921 " TERUKO 照子 1926

2 ND. DAUGHTER YOSHI ヨシ　1918 HUSBAND YOSHIMARU ABE 安部美丸 1914-2006

3RD. " SUMI スミ 1927-1976 " EIICHI OIKE 大池英一 1918-1996

The Homma family tree from Japan dates back 500 years. A
Buddhist temple in Chiba, Japan holds the records of the
births and deaths of the Homma family. Originally, the
Homma name was Honma. When Tomekichi Homma entered
Canada, the immigration officer misspelled his surname on the
application form.

Preface

Tomekichi Homma, a pioneer in the late 1800s, made a vital contribution to the Japanese community in Canada. This tale is as true as any can be when it has been passed down from one generation to another. Within these pages, you will read a fascinating collection of memories about Tomekichi, told by his children. It is the written record of one family's oral stories, to preserve the memory of their grandfather, great-grandfather, and great-great-grandfather. It has also been written so that others can learn about the extraordinary life of Tomekichi Homma.

In the late 1800s, many immigrant groups, such as the Chinese and East Indians, made their home in British Columbia. The Japanese, in particular, faced prejudice and hatred as they tried to make a life for themselves in Canada. This story describes what it was like for one Japanese man — Tomey — who immigrated to British Columbia during this time.

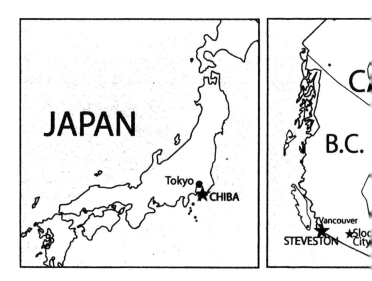

Introduction

This is the story of one remarkable man, Tomekichi Homma, and how his journey led him to become a significant Japanese Canadian pioneer. Tomekichi came to British Columbia as a Japanese immigrant during the late 1800s. His story unfolded during a time when discrimination, racial prejudice, and intolerance were commonly accepted, and anti-Asian attitudes were dominant and widespread. This is a disturbing and unforgettable period in British Columbia's history.

As a Japanese-Canadian citizen, Tomekichi Homma experienced the barbs of racial bigotry and injustice. He faced political and economic restrictions; he witnessed the racist law that prevented the Japanese from voting in any election. These encounters with intolerance and discrimination ignited Tomekichi's desire to help his fellow Japanese immigrants. His courage, commitment, and tenacity fuelled his crusade for justice and dignity for all. During his lifetime, Tomekichi worked tirelessly for the rights of the Japanese.

Today, Canadians have the distinction of living in a more tolerant and accepting society. The legacies of citizens such as Tomekichi Homma are that Canadians honour and celebrate many diverse cultural traditions and ethnic communities.

The maps illustrate Tomekichi Homma's journey to Canada and where he spent his lifetime.
(Janet Abe maps, 2003)

Chronology of Tomekichi Homma's Life

1865	Born on June 6 in Ichikawa, Japan.
1883	Age 18, arrived in Canada and settled in Richmond, British Columbia.
1887	Helped to establish the first Japanese Fishermen's Association in Steveston, and became its first president.
1887–1899	Held the position of president of the Japanese Fishermen's Association; helped to establish the Fishermen's Hospital and the first Japanese language school in Richmond.
1896	Became a naturalised Canadian citizen.
1897	Married Matsu Tanikawa of Fukuoka, Japan; moved to Vancouver, B.C.; helped to publish the Japanese language newsletter, *Dai Nippon;* manufactured and sold tofu; opened a Japanese restaurant; provided labourers for the CPR construction projects; founded a social club and served as its chairman.

1897	Opened a boarding house at the corner of Carrall and Pender in Vancouver, B.C. to help new Japanese immigrants.
1900–1902	Legally challenged the provincial government's law that denied the Japanese Canadians the right to vote; lost his court challenge when the Privy Council in London, England reversed earlier decisions that were in his favour.
1909	Moved to the Great Northern Fish Cannery in West Vancouver; worked as a night watchman at the cannery; co-owned waterfront property in North Vancouver; started a logging camp and sawmill in West Vancouver.
1915–1922	Conducted interviews for two books he wrote: *Treasures of Canada* and *An Appendix to the Directory of the Development of Japanese Canadians,* which were edited by Mr. Jinshiro Nakayama.
1929	Lost personal papers, photos, and diaries in a house fire at the cannery in West Vancouver; suffered two strokes and was bedridden.
1942 or 1943	Evacuated to Popoff, an internment settlement near Slocan City in the

interior of British Columbia, during World War II; separated from three of his children.

1945   Passed away on October 28, age 80, at Slocan and buried at Mountain View Cemetery in Vancouver, B.C.

1949   Tomekichi Homma's son Seiji attended the provincial legislature in Victoria, B.C.; he witnessed the changing of the law granting the Japanese the right to vote.

1951   Matsu passed away in West Vancouver and was buried next to Tomekichi.

1977   Mr. Rintaro Hayashi proposed that a school in Richmond, B.C., be named in honour of Tomekichi Homma.

1991   Tomekichi Homma Elementary School was officially opened in Richmond, B.C.

2002   The contributions of Tomekichi Homma as a prominent Japanese-Canadian pioneer were highlighted at the Nikkei Centre in Burnaby, B.C. during the 125th Anniversary of the First Japanese to Immigrate to Canada.

2003   Tomekichi Homma and his fight for

the right to vote were celebrated at the Japanese Canadian National Museum in Burnaby, B.C.

2004 An historical documentary was produced by Citytv Vancouver entitled "Local Heroes." Tomekichi Homma was one of three prominent citizens of British Columbia featured in this documentary.

In 1850, in a land far away lived a respected and wealthy family. For generations, the family known as Homma lived in the city now called Ichikawa in the ancient country of Japan. The Homma clan were samurai, the military class who served their lords with bravery and loyalty; they could trace their lineage back to the retainers of the Ashikaga shoguns in the 1400s. Each Homma patriarch devoutly followed the legacy of the samurai tradition.

Ancestors of the Homma family had been retainers of the powerful Kuroda Clan
(Abe family photo, date unknown)

During the 1800s, as head of the family, Masatada Homma raised each of his children in this tradition. As the Homma family grew, a fourth son was born in 1865. Masatada and his wife Chiyo became proud parents of a little boy whom they treasured and named Tomekichi (Tomey for short).

Growing up, Tomekichi observed as his father shaped the characters of his older brothers. His father inspired each son to do his best, even when faced with adversity. He raised them to follow the samurai code of conduct, to loyally serve one's family and community. From this, Tomey learned the meaning of courage, duty, and commitment.

Tomekichi's mother was also a samurai like his father. She was skilled with the long spear called a *naginata*. Samurai women often favoured this weapon to defend their homes. Mother Homma had such strength and dexterity with a naginata, that she could flip a one-kilogram bundle of hay clear over the house with precision!

In those days, Japanese custom dictated that elder sons must follow in their father's footsteps. Tomey's older brothers prepared to lead the Homma clan. Instead of carrying on the family tradition, Tomekichi chose a different path.

He was inquisitive and he yearned to learn about the world. Tomey's mother Chiyo, an aca-

okichi Genji Masaoki Homma, atriarch of his samurai clan, omekichi's father.
(Homma family photo, date unknown)

Chiyo Homma, Tomekichi's mother, also had a samurai lineage.
(Homma family photo, date unknown)

demic, became his tutor and taught him several languages. Tomey did not realise that by learning different languages he would develop a skill that would prove to be very useful later. Tomekichi thrived under his mother's guidance, and in time he too became an accomplished scholar.

Chiyo ensured that her youngest son's education was more than just book learning. She strongly believed in the Japanese proverb, "Learning is to man as the leaves and branches are to a tree." She wanted her son to develop mental discipline and a strong character like that of the samurai warrior, but she also fostered the traits of kindness, determination, and compassion. She understood the importance of serving the community, so, under his mother's capable instruction, Tomey acquired humility and a desire to help others. Chiyo's early influence helped shape the man Tomekichi would later become — a man of honour and integrity.

During the 1870s, life in Japan was harsh and difficult. Peasants working on farms were severely taxed, so many left their land and travelled to towns and cities in search of employment. Work was scarce and many men were jobless. A fortunate few were able to raise money for passage to other countries. These single, desperate men emigrated from Japan.

The first Japanese immigrants who arrived in British Columbia were poor, illiterate, and unable to speak English. These men were hired to perform jobs requiring hard physical labour; they toiled in sawmills, built the Canadian Pacific Railroad, cleared the land for farming, and worked on fishing boats. These Japanese workers desired success, and planned to return to Japan with their riches.

It was unusual for a cultured man such as Tomekichi to want to leave the comforts of his home and family, but he was restless and wanted to pursue his studies. With confidence, Tomey decided to sail to England to attend Oxford University. He boarded the ship with Yugoro Sekine, his lifelong friend; little did Tomey know that he would never see his family and homeland again. From the ship's deck, Tomey watched Japan disappear below the horizon. The thought of living in unknown surroundings excited the young man. When his ship docked for fresh supplies in British Columbia, Tomey revised his plans; he saw before him a land of promising opportunities. Tomekichi chose to stay in Canada to pursue a life of freedom and adventure.

When Tomekichi arrived in Canada in 1883, he was just eighteen years of age. With hope and anticipation, he wanted to succeed in his new land. He became one of the first Japanese to settle in Steveston, a small fishing village located at the mouth of the Fraser River in British Columbia.

An early view of Steveston's canneries. Tomekichi Homma was one of the first Japanese to settle here. Steveston became a growing Japanese community. *(CVA photo, 1890)*

The town of Steveston with the city wharf at the left.
(CVA photo, 1890)

In Steveston, Asians working in the fishing industry lived in tents near the river. This community was located on dry ground near the wharves and fish canneries. Here, Tomey was one of many who pitched a small canvas shelter where he slept each evening. Chinese and Japanese settlers lived side by side. This was Tomekichi's first home in Canada.

Tent city located near a cannery, early homes for the Japanese and Chinese workers in the fishing industry.
(IHHCM photo, ca. 1890)

For Tomey, life in the new frontier was foreign and strange. In Japan, Tomekichi led a privileged life, and he never had to work, but in Canada he needed to make a living to survive. Like most of the Japanese who had settled in Steveston, Tomekichi became a fisherman, too.

Fishing during this time was difficult. The boat Tomey worked on provided no shelter from hostile weather, and took on water in choppy seas. Its open construction offered no protection and exposed him to the elements.

Columbia River-type boats moored in Steveston
(Steves family photo, ca. 1900)

Many of the Japanese fishermen recognised Tomekichi as an educated man, strong in character, and a born leader. Tomey saw how the Japanese encountered hostility, racial prejudice, and discrimination. The anti-Asian sentiments affected and restricted all aspects of life for the Japanese immigrants. These attitudes motivated Tomey to work for change. He became an advocate for the Japanese immigrants in British Columbia.

During the late 1880s, Steveston was a thriving fishing port. Many of the Japanese who settled there were "people of the sea" and were recognised for their dedication to hard work. Japanese men worked on their boats and sold their catch to the canneries. Tomey felt that the fishing companies exploited the Japanese fishermen. The canneries paid the Japanese less for their catch than the Caucasians. Tomekichi realised that the discrimination against the Japanese fishermen would continue, unless they made changes in their industry. He knew they needed to improve

19

The thriving fishing industry in British Columbia, as shown in the early 1900s.
(Yesaki family photo, ca. 1900)

Fishermen in Columbia River-type boats, commonly used at that time. Tomekichi Homma would have fished in one of these.
(Steves family photo, 1908)

The Japanese Fishermen's Benevolent Society building. Tomekichi was the first president. The society's purpose was to improve the working conditions for the Japanese fishermen.
(CRA photo, ca. 1900)

their situation with the fishing companies by standing together in solidarity and negotiating a fair agreement. So, Tomey helped to establish the Japanese Fishermen's Association and became its first president. The association represented the fishermen as they strived to improve their working conditions and prosper in their work.

For the Japanese fishermen, living in Steveston was precarious. Their poor living conditions contributed to the spread of contagious diseases. Each summer, epidemics of typhoid fever affected many. So, it was not long before Tomekichi and others realised a health facility was needed to care for the Japanese fishermen and their families. Under Tomey's guidance, funds were raised to build a hospital. The Japanese fishermen paid yearly dues to support the medical facility, but everyone in the community, regardless of race, could receive free health care.

Tomekichi was instrumental in establishing the Japanese Fishermen's Hospital in Steveston. *(Steves family photo, ca. 1905)*

Tomey recognised the importance of educating the children in the growing Japanese community. At this time, Japanese children could not attend public schools in British Columbia. Educational authorities insisted there was no space to accommodate them. The Richmond School Board ruled that only those

Japanese children whose parents owned land in Richmond could attend the local schools. This eliminated the vast majority of Japanese families who were tenants in cannery houses and did not own land.

The hardworking Japanese people wanted their children to be educated, so that they could have a better life. Tomekichi supported the effort to start a school for these children. When the school opened, the immigrant children were instructed in the Japanese language. This preserved the language and customs of their parents.

It was important for the children to learn English, too. English-speaking teachers were hired to teach kindergarten. It was hoped the young children would readily acquire the new language and have the same educational success as their Caucasian peers. Several years later, Japanese students were allowed to register in British Columbia's public school system.

Tomekichi realised that learning the language of his new country was necessary if he wished to continue helping Japanese immigrants. Just as he had studied languages many years before, now he strived to learn English. Soon Tomey became known for his competency in English. Many of the Japanese and Chinese immigrants were illiterate, so they sought his assistance. Tomey translated newspapers, read and wrote letters for the Chinese and Japanese immigrants, and assisted in the courts as an interpreter. Rarely could the new immigrants afford to pay for this service, but Tomey always accepted the task.

After living in Canada for thirteen years, Tomekichi was very proud when he became a naturalised Canadian citizen in 1896. Tomey assumed that by becoming a Canadian citizen, he would have the same rights as all others, but he soon

Staff and patients at the Japanese Fishermen's Hospital; care was provided to those in the community.
(CRA photo, 1897)

23

learned Japanese Canadians were not allowed to vote in British Columbia. This inequity bothered Tomekichi greatly and he vowed to change the law.

In 1897, Tomekichi moved to Vancouver to run a boarding house in the thriving Japanese community. There, a close friend introduced Tomey to Matsu Tanikawa, a headstrong, unattached, young woman who came to Canada against her parents' wishes. The marriage was arranged, and the couple wed. Unlike Tomey, Matsu did not have a samurai ancestry, nor was she from a cultured, aristocratic family. In Japan, their marriage would not have been approved.

Matsu was a farmer's daughter, so she understood the difficulties and uncertainty that came with farming. Her childhood experiences in Japan prepared her to survive the hardships and sacrifices she would later face in British Columbia.

Early in their marriage, Matsu learned the importance of her husband's commitment to the Japanese community. She was willing and ready to assist her new husband. As new Vancouver residents, Matsu and Tomekichi travelled by horse and buggy to visit the Steveston community. Their journey took a full day. Sometimes, the young couple spent the night with friends before returning home the next day.

From his personal experience, Tomekichi knew how difficult it was for new Japanese immigrants to

find employment and a place to live. He became a labour contractor, finding jobs for new immigrants with the CPR (Canadian Pacific Railway). As more Japanese arrived and settled in Vancouver, Tomey rented out rooms in his boarding house on the corner of Carrall and Pender Streets. It became known that Tomekichi offered free lodging and meals to new immigrants if they were penniless, so many found their way to his establishment. Numerous individuals benefited from Tomekichi's generosity and good will.

While living in Vancouver, Tomekichi read the

Dupont (now known as Pender St.) and Carrall Streets. Tomekichi resided at 37 Dupont St. During this time, he started his legal struggle, 1900–1902.
(CVA, ca. 1900)

25

local English newspapers. He realised that as the Japanese-Canadian community grew, a newspaper written in their language was needed. This would enable the Japanese to read about their community, learn about current events, and read news from back home. The first issue of the *Dai Nippon* was published in 1897; Tomey was on the first board of directors. This bi-monthly newsletter was circulated and well received.

Asians experienced many barriers and inequalities in British Columbia during the late 1800s. They were:

- unable to vote in municipal, provincial, and federal elections;
- not allowed to work in the professions of law and pharmacy;
- barred from other occupations, such as police work, the forestry service, post office employment, and public health nursing;
- unable to buy or work on crown land (land owned by the government); and
- not allowed to serve as a jury member or hold public office.

Tomey felt these restrictions were unjust and intolerable. He wanted to be a true citizen of Canada. He realised how important it was for the Japanese to have the right to vote and to be treated as equals in Canadian society. Tomekichi decided to challenge the Provincial Voters' Act that prevented Asians from voting.

On October 19, 1900, he travelled to a polling station in Vancouver. Purposefully, Tomey proceeded to the front entrance, aware that what he was about to do would attract attention and controversy. With quiet courage, Tomekichi asked to have his name added to the Provincial Voters' List. Immediately, Thomas Cunningham, the returning officer in charge, refused; Tomekichi's request was against the law.

The *Victoria Colonist,* a local newspaper reported the following, "We are relieved from the possibility of having polling booths swamped by a horde of Orientals who are totally unfit...to exercise the ballot, and whose voting would completely demoralize politics." This was the public attitude of the day.

Six days later, Tomekichi filed a lawsuit. He knew his application would challenge and test the racist law. Harris and Bull, a Vancouver law firm, accepted the case and agreed to represent Tomey. This prompted immediate media attention and government reaction. The local English newspapers reported Tomekichi's case. One headline read, "Jap Tries to Get His Name on the Voters' List in Vancouver." Cunningham stated to reporters that he would put no Asiatic name on the Voters' List. He would go to jail first.

Tomey faced some criticism within the Japanese community for his legal action. Tensions rose, as some believed his conduct was foolish and would result in the provincial government making the lives of the Japanese more difficult. But Tomey was determined; he ignored the criticisms from his fellow Japanese Canadians and persevered with his campaign. Others recognised the importance of Tomey's cause, and they established a trust fund to help pay his legal costs. The majority of the Japanese community supported Tomekichi and gave him the strength to continue.

Tomey's struggle on behalf of the Japanese

JAPANESE WILL FIGHT

IN THE CANADIAN COURTS

FOR REGISTRATION AS VOTER

To the Collector of Votes of the Riding of Vancouver city electoral district:

I hereby give you notice that on the 7th day of November, 1900, before the county court of Vancouver to be holden at Vancouver, I intend to have reviewed your decision made on the 19th day of October, 1900, whereby you disallowed the name of Tomey Homma to be placed on the register of votes for the riding of Vancouver electoral district.

Dated the twenty-fifth day of October, 1900.

(Signed)　　　　TOMEY HOMMA,

Boarding house keeper and employment agent residing at lane at rear of 37 Dupont street, in the city of Vancouver, by his solicitors.

(Signed)　　　HARRIS & BULL,

Bank of B. N. A. building, Vancouver.

The naturalized Japanese are evidently going to get on the voters' list if they can. The above notification received by Collector of Votes Thomas Cunningham yesterday indicate that they mean business. The man Homma is but one whose name the collector of votes has refused to add to the list, and his will most probably be made a test case.

In Tuesday's issue of The Province the exclusive announcement was made that the Japanese Association of Vancouver had decided in meeting that those of their race who were naturalized, had the right to be put on the list, and to vote in the coming elections.

In a conversation last evening the collector stated flatly that he would put no Asiatic name on the voters' list. He would "go to jail first," he said. No matter what happened—courts or no courts, orders or no orders—the present collector of votes will not add one name of a Chinaman or Japanese to the voters' list, the preparation of which he now has in hand.

The year after confederation, according to Mr. Cunningham, the old Franchise act was passed which was subsequently repealed in 1897, bringing the voters on to the provincial lists. The Provincial act expressly legislates against Japanese, Chinese and Indians going on the lists and imposes a fine of $50 to be levied on summary conviction before any magistrate on any collector who adds the name of a Chinaman, Japanese or Indian to the provincial voters list.

The act does not state that these people may not vote—it does not say that they shall not be placed on the list, and that only men whose names are on the list are entitled to vote, so the effect is achieved in that manner.

What might happen should the thousands of Japanese who have lately been naturalized have their names placed on the list, can only be left to conjecture.

In the meanwhile Collector Cunningham stands firm.

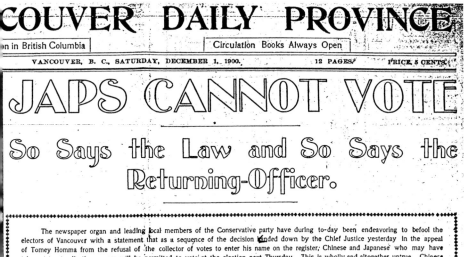

JAPS CANNOT VOTE

So Says the Law and So Says the Returning-Officer.

The newspaper organ and leading local members of the Conservative party have during to-day been endeavoring to befool the electors of Vancouver with a statement that as a sequence of the decision handed down by the Chief Justice yesterday in the appeal of Tomey Homma from the refusal of the collector of votes to enter his name on the register, Chinese and Japanese who may have taken out naturalization papers will be permitted to vote at the election next Thursday. This is wholly and altogether untrue. Chinese and Japanese will not be permitted to vote then or at any other time in British Columbia. The sole right which is secured to them under the Chief Justice's decision is to have their names entered on the new provincial roll, which, as everyone is well aware, is not to be used at all in the present election. To make matters doubly sure, Deputy Returning Officer Duncan, in the absence of Returning Officer McGregor in the north, has issued explicit instructions to all deputies not to permit any Japanese, Chinese or Indians to mark a ballot. There is little doubt in the minds of all who have gone into the case that the present proceedings are merely the outcroppings of as daring and disreputable a Tory plot as ever disgraced the political history of Canada. Mr. Maxwell will probably have something to tell the public under this head at the big meeting which he addresses this evening at the Theatre Royal.

became a two-year legal battle requiring great stamina, patience, and courage. He was confident that his cause was just, and he expected his challenge to succeed. If victorious, he believed other minorities, such as Chinese and East Indian immigrants, would also achieve the right to vote, and more Canadian citizens would be treated in a fair and democratic manner.

At first, the case went to a lower court in British Columbia, which favoured Tomey in its decision, but the government did not agree with this and appealed to the Supreme Court of B.C. The Supreme Court upheld the previous court's decision. The provincial government was dismayed by the outcome and, as a last resort, took the case to the Privy Council in England.

Tomekichi was greatly disappointed and discouraged when he learned that his case had been overturned by the Privy Council. The Japanese would still be denied the right to vote. The Council's

Reaction to Asians seeking the right to vote.
(The Vancouver Daily Province, December 1900)

Announcement of Tomekichi's attempt to get his name registered on the voters' list.
(The Vancouver Daily Province, October 1900)

29

Family portrait.
(Homma family photo, ca. 1909)

30

decision was difficult for Tomey to understand. It meant that the Japanese would remain as second-class citizens in Canada.

In 1909, Tomekichi and Matsu decided to leave the bustling city of Vancouver. They moved with their children across the inlet to West Vancouver. Tomey was employed at the Great Northern Fish Cannery as a night watchman. West Vancouver was a quiet, waterfront settlement surrounded by rugged mountains and forests. Travelling was difficult and dangerous. One narrow, gravel lane led part of the way to the cannery; for the remaining distance, travellers had to hike along the shoreline. When the tide was high, it was strenuous to wade through the cold, numbing ocean.

The Great Northern Fish Cannery was "a walled city" in an isolated area of West Vancouver. The Hommas became one of the first families to live in this self-sufficient community of workers. The cannery contained its own general store, a smokehouse, and a mess hall. Chinese, Japanese, and Aboriginal seasonal workers occupied bunkhouses. The cabins were reserved for families, such as the Hommas, who lived at the cannery year round. When Tomey travelled from the cannery to Vancouver, he often carried a pistol as a safety precaution.

NO JAPANESE NEED APPLY TO BE VOTERS

Privy Council Has Decided Against the Full Court and Declares That British Columbia May Refuse to Enroll Orientals.

The Privy Council of Great Britain has reversed the decision of the Full Court in British Columbia, and has decided that it is within the power of the Legislature of the province to prevent Japanese from voting.

This news was received in Vancouver to-day in a telegram to Messrs. Wilson, Senkler & Bloomfield, Mr. Charles Wilson, K. C., having been counsel for the province in its contention that Japanese should not be allowed to vote, and it was he who had most to do with the preparation of the case for submission to the judicial committee of the Privy Council.

The case of Tommy Homa, the test action of the Japanese in their fight for voting powers, has been before the courts for a year and a half. Tommy Homa was a resident of Vancouver, and a naturalized British subject, and he applied to the Collector of Voters in Vancouver to have his name placed on the list, but the Collector refused. He took this stand on the ground furnished by a section in the Electoral Act, which provides that no Chinese, Japanese or Indian shall have his name placed on the list.

Final court decision regarding Tomekichi Homma's case.
(The Vancouver Daily Province, *December 1902*)

Map of the Great
Northern Cannery prior
to 1927.
(Moe Yesaki, 2003)

Great Northern Cannery
before 1927

Houses for Japanese families, such as the Hommas, who
resided year round at the cannery.
(Millerd family photo, 1918)

33

All the neighbourhood children gathered together at the cannery. When the fishing season was over, they had access to all the buildings where they could play hide and seek, roller hockey, and tag.
(Homma family photo, 1927)

Tomekichi's children enjoyed a wonderful, carefree childhood. He believed each of his children would grow up and become responsible, independent adults and find their place in life.
(Homma family photo, 1935)

At the cannery, the Homma children lived at the beach all summer. They played, fished, and made rafts from driftwood; being around water, the children had to be proficient swimmers.
(Homma Family, ca. 1926)

Wintertime the children sledded, skated, and built snowmen. Year round, they chummed around in groups; they were always playing with someone.
(Homma family photo, ca. 1927)

35

Starting a new life at the cannery was a struggle for the Homma family. It was difficult to feed and clothe their five sons and two daughters. The family turned to the ocean for food, harvesting clams, trapping crabs, and netting smelts. At five o'clock each morning, the children paddled their rowboats to check their nets and traps, collecting their catch. Whatever they caught would be their dinner that evening.

During the summers, the children were sent to pick blackberries, wild strawberries, huckleberries, and salmon berries for jams and jellies. As the children walked home with full buckets, cars stopped and strangers offered twenty-five cents for the berries. The youngsters always declined, for they would rather enjoy their mother's sweet jams throughout the winter.

Food was not plentiful, so it was never wasted. The Homma children were taught that each grain of rice served must be eaten. Every day the children received simple meals; special treats could not be afforded. The youngsters were especially delighted when their father translated newspapers and wrote

Children living at the cannery had to be transported to school by bus or train. Tomekichi's youngest son, Keay, was often the only Asian student in his class.
(Homma family photo, ca. 1927)

The Homma house at the Great Northern Cannery. The window on the left was Tomekichi's bedroom. He had a single picture hanging on the wall by his bed; it was a large, coloured portrait of the King and Queen of England.
(Homma family photo, 1930)

The shoreline by the Great Northern Cannery.
(Millerd family photo, date unknown)

letters home for the Chinese labourers and cooks because he received pies, cakes, and other sweets as gifts. The family appreciated invitations from the Chinese workers to attend feasts at their bunkhouse.

The band of Homma children was well known to all those living at the cannery. The girls were quiet, polite, and well behaved. The Homma boys were naughty and mischievous rascals. On most days Matsu went to people's homes to apologise for the behaviour of her *yuncha bozus* (active little boys). On each of these countless occasions when the boys got out of hand and made trouble, Tomekichi always chose never to strike his children; not one of them, not once, not ever.

Like his mother before him, Tomey taught his children kindness and compassion for others. They often heard their father say, "You don't pick on the weak; you help them." Tomey set an example for his children, as they often observed him helping others. This was an important lesson in the Homma household, and the children were reprimanded if they forgot.

All the Homma youngsters learned to speak English and Japanese. Tomey and Matsu wanted their children to learn both languages so they could live comfortably in either culture. The Hommas believed that Canadian customs and traditions were important, but they also wanted their children to understand the heritage and history of Japan.

Chinese bunkhouse
(Millerd Family photo, 1918)

38

When Tomekichi was living at the cannery, he still made frequent trips to Vancouver for meetings and social events. He also received many visitors at his home. Tomekichi is sitting in the top left corner.
(Homma family photo, ca. 1914)

While growing up, the Homma children saw little of their hard-working father during the spring and summer. As Tomekichi's reputation as an advocate grew, he was often asked to help the Japanese community in Vancouver. The children remember seeing more of their father during fall and winter, when days were short and the weather made travelling treacherous. Tomey always tried to be home before nightfall; this enabled him to spend time with his family. The children have cherished memories of special times spent with him.

One such memory was the annual chopping of the family Christmas tree. As the children roamed the forest searching for the perfect tree, Tomey would hide, later jumping out pretending to be a bear. Screams and laughter echoed through the woods as the children scattered.

After dinner each evening, Tomekichi gathered his family around the pot-bellied stove to hear his stories of samurai, feudal lords, and battles. Seven youngsters raptly listened, imagining life in far-away Japan. Moans and groans escaped from the children when their father abruptly announced, "Enough tonight. We do again tomorrow."

To end each evening, the troop of Homma children scrambled to line up, shoulder to shoulder, imitating their father as he did his nightly callisthenics. Tomekichi believed in the age-old saying, "Strong body; strong mind."

Tomey also entertained the cannery children. One favourite pastime was play fighting like samurai. The children battled, sticks waving, voices shouting, with chaos everywhere. Slowly Tomekichi rose and explained, "You don't do it like that. You do it like this." His demonstrations of fighting ended with the traditional samurai warrior scream, *"Keiye!"*

Watching carefully, the children copied his actions, completely unaware of his noble samurai background. Years later, when the Homma children were adults, they learned of their samurai ancestry. The stories Tomekichi had told his children for countless years were often those of his own family history.

Not only did Tomey relish telling stories, he spent hours each day reading. Books, magazines, newspapers, and other reading material in Japanese and English cluttered their home. Tomekichi's strong desire for knowledge remained with him throughout his life.

His children also remember their father's keen interest in writing. On many occasions they witnessed their father hunched over a table, brush or pen in hand, writing letters and *haiku* (Japanese poetry), and practising Japanese calligraphy. Papers were scattered about; dark ink spots stained his hands.

The Homma family sitting in front of their winter supply of wood for their stove. Tomekichi and Matsu had eight children; of these, six survived. An infant girl died from a fever in 1903. A son died in a drowning accident in 1913.
(Homma family photo, 1921)

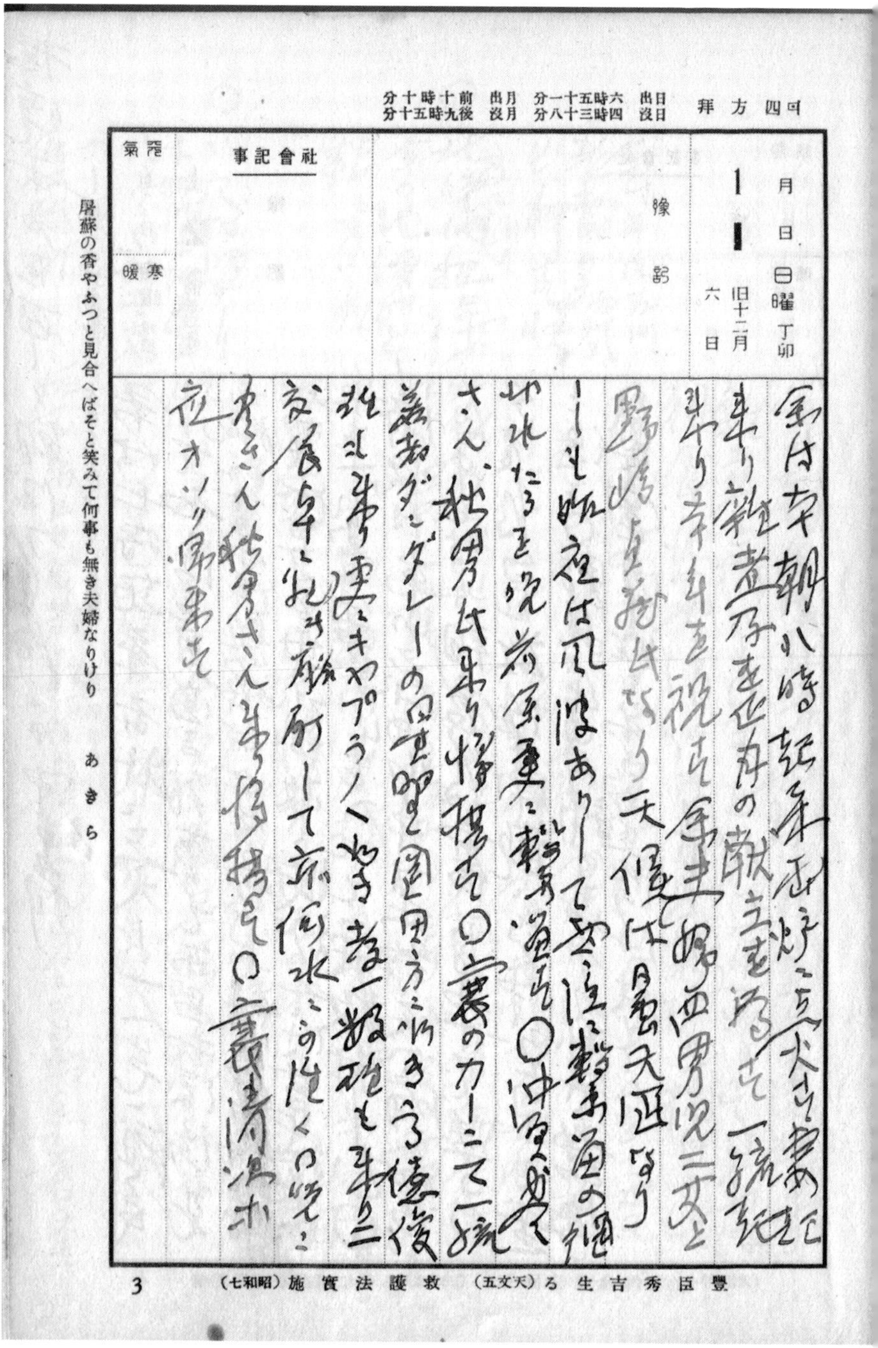
四方拝　日出 六時五十一分　日没 四時三十八分　月出 前十時十分　月没 後九時五十分

1 月 日 日曜 丁卯　旧十二月 六日

豫記

社會記事

氣溫　寒暖

屠蘇の香やふつと見合へばそと笑みて何事も無き夫婦なりけり　あきら

豊臣秀吉生る（天文五）　救護法實施（昭和七）　3

Page taken from the last remaining diary of Tomekichi dated January 1, 1933. He wrote in an old classical Japanese style; his writings reflected family activities and daily life. *(Homma family, 1933)*

Writing in his diary was an anticipated daily activity. The children knew not to bother their father when he was writing. Tomekichi described what life was like in the Japanese immigrant community and he recorded the names of those who first accomplished a notable achievement or obtained success. Their home was filled with stacks of diaries on the floor, on shelves, and in boxes throughout the house.

For years, Tomekichi created scrapbooks with newspaper clippings about important current events. These were placed in chronological order and neatly stacked on bookshelves that lined the walls of his bedroom. People at the cannery remember Tomey meticulously cutting and pasting articles for his scrapbooks. He collected information about current affairs and articles that he deemed of interest. These scrapbooks became historical documents of the times.

Unfortunately, in 1929, most of Tomekichi's personal papers, diaries, and files were lost in a house fire at the cannery. His extensive collection of photographs and books all perished. Today, little remains of his personal possessions.

By the time Tomey was fifty years old, he wanted to retire and enjoy life with his family at the Great Northern Fish Cannery. As a leader within the Japanese community, he was respected and held in high esteem. But retirement was not to be. Asian immigrants continued to seek Tomey and ask for his advice. Matsu complained that Tomey's volunteer work took him away from home frequently. It became necessary for her to become the primary breadwinner, so she worked as a housekeeper while Tomey continued with his community activism.

The Hommas on the lawn of the Sigmore family property in West Vancouver on the day of Seiji's high school graduation. Matsu was their housekeeper and learned to cook English-style food.
(Homma family photo, 1925)

Matsu understood the necessity of her husband's work and accepted the hardships it brought her family. She was a dutiful wife and mother who held the family together with heart and determination.

When the children were young, Matsu laboured collecting the logs that washed up on the beach. She sawed and chopped them, so they could be used in the fireplace and the wood-burning stove. This physically demanding job made her back and arms ache, and her hands calloused.

Without the convenience of running water, Matsu had to collect water from a spring five blocks away. The spring water came from a hole dug in the ground; men had lined the bottom and sides of the

Beached logs would be used for firewood to heat homes.
(Millerd family photo, 1918)

hole with wood to keep the water from becoming murky and gritty. The water was always ice-cold, even on the hottest summer day. Again and again, Matsu walked to and from the spring carrying water in two buckets tied to the ends of a long pole that rested across her shoulders. Clean water was needed for cooking, drinking, bathing, and other uses; such strenuous jobs were her daily responsibility.

While looking after the home, Matsu faced constant obstacles. The Hommas owned chickens that roamed freely in their front yard. One day, when eagles circled above them, Matsu hollered, banged pots, and waved her arms. But her actions did nothing to discourage one bold eagle from swooping down and snatching a chicken with its sharp talons. Losing even one bird meant Matsu had to struggle to keep her family fed.

While Matsu looked after the family, Tomekichi began to gather information for two books documenting the lives of the first Japanese immigrants in Canada. Mr. Jinshiro Nakayama edited the books. Tomey's research and writing ensured success for this project. However, it meant he would be away from his family for several months at a time. His eldest daughter, Yoshi, recalled the times her mother complained when their father travelled throughout British Columbia. During these absences, Tomey interviewed thousands of early Japanese immigrants. He did not realise that it would take seven years of hard work to finish the project. The books, *Canada no Hoko (Treasures of Canada)* and *Canada Doho Hatten Taikan Furoku (An Appendix to the Directory of the Development of Japanese Canadians),* were finally completed in 1922.

Matsu with her ikebana arrangement outside of their home. She loved flowers and spent time tending to her gardens.
(Homma family photo, 1934)

The elderly Tomekichi outside of his home at the cannery after his first stroke.
(Homma family photo, 1934)

As Tomekichi aged, he sought fulfilment and joy in the ordinary rituals of life. He spent his spare time playing a game of Japanese chess called *shogi*. This game required patience, logic, and careful planning. If no one was available to play chess with him, Tomey played against himself. During fishing season, six or seven men from the cannery visited the Homma house. Each man quietly waited his turn to play chess against Tomey.

A landscape photo of the Great Northern Cannery in 1939, before the Hommas were evacuated to an internment camp. *(Aero Surveys)*

Police Instructed: Japs Must Carry Cards

Registration Being Checked

Instructions have been sent out to all provincial and municipal police, and to army, naval and air force officers to stop every Japanese on the street and demand his or her identification and registration card, the Royal Canadian Mounted Police informed The Sun today.

The instructions are part of a widespread drive to check on those who have tried to escape registration.

The Japanese must produce a yellow card if he is a national; a white card if he is Canadian born or a pink card if he is naturalized.

Until last Saturday, January 10, registration of Japanese was voluntary. That was under Defense of Canada Regulations.

On Sunday, January 11, Order-in-Council No. 9760 came into effect, making it compulsory. The Japs are now given until February 7 to register and thereafter they will be subject to severe penalties for failure to do so.

"Now we have a chance to get up with those who haven't registered," said The Sun's informant today.

"Are there many," he was asked.

"We have a few on our list. I can't give you the figure. Our biggest headache is the

changing of names. If a J married into a family where there is no other man, he automatically takes the name of his bride, so that if there a any children here name is c ried on. It is a Japanese c tom. You can see how hard is to check."

Some 200 Japs per day are istering at the RCMP barra in Vancouver.

Failure to register carried fine of $200 or three months jail, or both. Thereafter alien would be interned for ation of the war. Burder proof that he has registered with the alien, not the arres officer.

On the weekends, Tomekichi was surrounded with family and friends. The Hommas were the first family at the cannery to own a radio. People gathered in the cramped parlour each week to listen to the broadcast of the Saturday night hockey game. Everyone, including the children, understood that this was the time to listen; no talking or noise was ever permitted.

Tomey enjoyed walking in solitude along the shoreline each morning at dawn. This was his time for quiet reflection. Sometimes, his youngest son Keay accompanied him. Together they placed rocks on logs that they thought would be suitable for firewood; later, family members walked to the beach to chop their claimed wood. These routines gave order and purpose to each day. Tomekichi was content; life at the cannery was peaceful.

❀

Then an event took place that changed the lives of all Japanese living in British Columbia. On December 7, 1941, Japan bombed Pearl Harbour in Hawaii and entered the Second World War. Canada declared war on Japan. This event intensified the hatred and racist attitudes held by many against the Japanese in British Columbia. Widespread propaganda scared some into believing that Japanese Canadians would be loyal to Japan and pose a security risk to Canada. This unfounded fear pressured the government to declare all men, women, and children of Japanese descent as "enemy aliens."

The government of Canada bowed to public

During the Second World War, the Japanese in Canada were identified as enemy aliens and required to register and carry an identification card. (Vancouver Sun, *January 1942*)

pressure and rounded up the Japanese and sent them to internment camps far from the West Coast. Japanese Canadians were forced to leave their personal belongings, homes, and businesses to relocate to internment camps. Some Japanese were given twenty-four hours notice; families were allowed to take only two pieces of luggage. Many families were directed to Hastings Park in Vancouver before being transferred to other areas of Canada. Here, they were made to live in the livestock pens. Evacuees were forced onto trains and sent to the interior of British Columbia. Others were sent to the prairies to work as labourers on sugar beet farms. Men were separated from their families, and sent to camps to build roads. This was an anxious and painful time as everyone was uprooted.

A Caucasian man named Bunny McBride lived near the Great Northern Fish Cannery, and grew up with many of the Japanese children. He shared his perspective about the Japanese relocation, "They just disappeared. We didn't even have a chance to say good-bye to them."

By this time, many citizens of British Columbia knew the name of Tomekichi Homma. He was widely acknowledged for his leadership within the Japanese community and for his legal challenge to the Provincial Voters' Act. Tomey's distinguished reputation led the British Columbia Security Commission to offer the Hommas a private railway car to transport them to the internment camp. This proposal to travel in comfort and luxury as privileged citizens was immediately refused. The elderly couple joined their fellow exiles and travelled together on the crowded train.

Announcement that Japanese living on the West Coast must leave their homes, which eventually led to their relocation to internment camps.
(Vancouver Sun, January 1942)

Japs Accept Ottawa Order Calmly; Total to Leave Homes in Doubt

Vancouver Japanese are taking the news that came from Ottawa Wednesday quietly, ██████ though there is some disquietude as many face the probability of having to leave their homes here and go to other parts, the general disposition is to await further and more definite news.

It is impossible, until details are known, to estimate the number who may have to move.

In the whole province there are approximately 6000 "nationals" which means Japan-born who have not become naturalized Canadian citizens.

About 4000 of these are men who, if they are in what are designated as "protected areas" will have to move.

But until it is known just what these "protected areas" are to be, and whether their woman are to be included, leading Japanese refuse to estimate how many of them may have to move.

There is much speculation as to whether "nationals" in the Fraser Valley will be included.

WARNED TO KEEP COOL

A Japanese spokesman said he expected to see a large response to the announcement of formation of a volunteer civilian corps of Japanese Canadians. Many have been volunteering for some time to serve Canada "in any way they can."

"The New Canadian," the English-speaking Japanese newspaper, published late Wednesday an appeal to all Japanese headed "Keep Cool and Keep Calm." It said:

"Keep cool and keep calm and don't get excited!

"Let's wait until all the details of the new regulations are worked out before we start rushing around like a flock of chickens with their heads off.

"Ottawa's announcement is only the general plan of what is

ment has stressed that principles of justice and fair treatment must be maintained.

"The administration of these regulations, we ████ will therefore be conducted in a common sense manner and with the proper regard for these principles.

"Let's not jump to the silliest extreme conclusions and get ourselves just balled up with over-worked nerves. And if we must talk about the 'situation' we'll feel better if we don't say anything unless we know what we are talking about.

"Reliable information on all the details will be forthcoming soon, so in the meantime let's keep cool and calm."

Officers of the RCMP were still without any word from Ottawa today and are not expecting any "for another day or two."

READY TO START WORK

Mr. Justice Sidney A. Smith, named to the three-man committee which will supervise transfers of the interned Japanese fishing fleet to non-Japanese operators, expects the committee to start functioning immediately after arrival of Commander B. L. Johnson, RCNVR, from Ottawa.

Commander Johnson, according to private advices, will reach Vancouver on Monday

51

NOTICE

TO ALL PERSONS OF JAPANESE RACIAL ORIGIN

Having reference to the Protected Area of British Columbia as described in an Extra of the Canada Gazette, No. 174 dated Ottawa, Monday, February 2, 1942:-

1. EVERY PERSON OF THE JAPANESE RACE, WHILE WITHIN THE PROTECTED AREA AFORESAID, SHALL HEREAFTER BE AT HIS USUAL PLACE OF RESIDENCE EACH DAY BEFORE SUNSET AND SHALL REMAIN THEREIN UNTIL SUNRISE ON THE FOLLOWING DAY, AND NO SUCH PERSON SHALL GO OUT OF HIS USUAL PLACE OF RESIDENCE AFORESAID UPON THE STREETS OR OTHERWISE DURING THE HOURS BETWEEN SUNSET AND SUNRISE;

2. NO PERSON OF THE JAPANESE RACE SHALL HAVE IN HIS POSSESSION OR USE IN SUCH PROTECTED AREA ANY MOTOR VEHICLE, CAMERA, RADIO TRANSMITTER, RADIO RECEIVING SET, FIREARM, AMMUNITION OR EXPLOSIVE;

3. IT SHALL BE THE DUTY OF EVERY PERSON OF THE JAPANESE RACE HAVING IN HIS POSSESSION OR UPON HIS PREMISES ANY ARTICLE MENTIONED IN THE NEXT PRECEDING PARAGRAPH, FORTHWITH TO CAUSE SUCH ARTICLE TO BE DELIVERED UP TO ANY JUSTICE OF THE PEACE RESIDING IN OR NEAR THE LOCALITY WHERE ANY SUCH ARTICLE IS HAD IN POSSESSION, OR TO AN OFFICER OR CONSTABLE OF THE POLICE FORCE OF THE PROVINCE OR CITY IN OR NEAR SUCH LOCALITY OR TO AN OFFICER OR CONSTABLE OF THE ROYAL CANADIAN MOUNTED POLICE.

4. ANY JUSTICE OF THE PEACE OR OFFICER OR CONSTABLE RECEIVING ANY ARTICLE MENTIONED IN PARAGRAPH 2 OF THIS ORDER SHALL GIVE TO THE PERSON DELIVERING THE SAME A RECEIPT THEREFOR AND SHALL REPORT THE FACT TO THE COMMISSIONER OF THE ROYAL CANADIAN MOUNTED POLICE, AND SHALL RETAIN OR OTHERWISE DISPOSE OF ANY SUCH ARTICLE AS DIRECTED BY THE SAID COMMISSIONER.

5. ANY PEACE OFFICER OR ANY OFFICER OR CONSTABLE OF THE ROYAL CANADIAN MOUNTED POLICE HAVING POWER TO ACT AS SUCH PEACE OFFICER OR OFFICER OR CONSTABLE IN THE SAID PROTECTED AREA, IS AUTHORIZED TO SEARCH WITHOUT WARRANT THE PREMISES OR ANY PLACE OCCUPIED OR BELIEVED TO BE OCCUPIED BY ANY PERSON OF THE JAPANESE RACE REASONABLY SUSPECTED OF HAVING IN HIS POSSESSION OR UPON HIS PREMISES ANY ARTICLE MENTIONED IN PARAGRAPH 2 OF THIS ORDER, AND TO SEIZE ANY SUCH ARTICLE FOUND ON SUCH PREMISES;

6. EVERY PERSON OF THE JAPANESE RACE SHALL LEAVE THE PROTECTED AREA AFORESAID FORTHWITH;

7. NO PERSON OF THE JAPANESE RACE SHALL ENTER SUCH PROTECTED AREA EXCEPT UNDER PERMIT ISSUED BY THE ROYAL CANADIAN MOUNTED POLICE;

8. IN THIS ORDER, "PERSONS OF THE JAPANESE RACE" MEANS, AS WELL AS ANY PERSON WHOLLY OF THE JAPANESE RACE, A PERSON NOT WHOLLY OF THE JAPANESE RACE IF HIS FATHER OR MOTHER IS OF THE JAPANESE RACE AND IF THE COMMISSIONER OF THE ROYAL CANADIAN MOUNTED POLICE BY NOTICE IN WRITING HAS REQUIRED OR REQUIRES HIM TO REGISTER PURSUANT TO ORDER-IN-COUNCIL P.C. 9760 OF DECEMBER 16th, 1941.

DATED AT OTTAWA THIS 26th DAY OF FEBRUARY, 1942.

Louis S. St. Laurent,
Minister of Justice

To be posted in a Conspicuous Place

TO MALE ENEMY ALIENS
NOTICE

Under date of February 2nd, 1942, the Honourable the Minister of National Defence with the concurrence of the Minister of Justice gave public notice defining an area of British Columbia, as described below, to be a protected area after the 31st day of January, 1942; that is to say, that area of the Province of British Columbia, including all islands, west of a line described hereunder:-

Commencing at boundary point No. 7 on the International Boundary between the Dominion of Canada and Alaska, thence following the line of the "Cascade Mountains" as defined by paragraph 2 of Section 24 of the Interpretation Act of British Columbia, being Chapter 1 of the Revised Statutes of 1936, to the Northwest corner of Lot 13-10, Range 5, Coast Land Districts, thence due East to a point due North of the Northwest corner of Lot 373, Range 5, Coast Land District, thence due South to said Northwest corner of Lot 373 being a point on the aforementioned line of the "Cascade Mountains", (being the area surrounding the village municipality of Terrace); thence following said line of the "Cascade Mountains" to the Western Boundary of Township 5, Range 26, West of the 6th Meridian, thence following the Northerly, Easterly and Southerly Boundaries of said Township 5, to the Southwest corner thereof, being a point on the line of the "Cascade Mountains" (being the area surrounding the village municipality of Hope); thence following the "Cascade Mountains" to the Southerly boundary of the Province.

Pursuant to the provisions of Regulation 4 of the Defence of Canada Regulations, the Minister of Justice has, on the 5th day of February, 1942, ordered that:-

1. All male Enemy Aliens of the ages of 18 years to 45 years, inclusive, shall leave the protected area hereinbefore referred to on or before the 1st day of April, 1942;

2. That, subject to the provisions of paragraph No. 1 of this Order, no Enemy Alien shall, after the date of this order, enter, leave or return to such protected area except with the permission of the Commissioner of the Royal Canadian Mounted Police Force, or an Officer of that Force designated by the Commissioner to act for him in this respect;

3. That no Enemy Alien shall have in his possession or use, while in such protected area, any camera, radio transmitter, radio short-wave receiving set, firearm, ammunition, or explosive.

OTTAWA, February 7, 1942.

S.T. WOOD (Commissioner)
Royal Canadian Mounted Police

TO BE POSTED IN A CONSPICUOUS PLACE

A temporary living quarter designated for Japanese women at Hastings Park in Vancouver (PNE grounds). Husbands and wives were segregated before being sent on to the internment camps.
(Alec Eastwood Collection, 1942)

The men's dormitory at Hastings Park offered little privacy. It was the clearing station before the men were relocated across Canada. *(VPL, 1942)*

This photo of Tomekichi Homma was taken for his registration card.
(Homma family photo, 1941)

This photo of Matsu Homma was taken for her registration card.
(Homma family photo, 1941)

Tomekichi and Matsu, their eldest son and his family, and the two youngest Homma children were relocated to Popoff in the Slocan Valley, in British Columbia. This was one of the newly built settlements for the internees. Their other three children were dispersed to internment camps throughout the interior of British Columbia.

At first, tents served as temporary homes until small wooden huts covered with black tar paper were constructed. Initially, the huts lacked insulation, heating, electricity, and running water. During the severe winters, the huts were bitterly cold with ice forming between wooden boards, on the heads of nails, and inside each window. When fires were lit, the ice thawed, and water ran down and puddled on the floors. Rags were placed along the base of walls to soak up the dripping water.

Summers were unbearably hot and humid. To stay cool, families swam at a nearby river and Slocan Lake. Older Japanese took to shady patches with their fans. Summer vegetable gardens were needed and carefully tended to help feed families over winter. A tin can with holes punched in the bottom was used for watering.

Tomekichi Homma's efforts to improve human rights and the dignity of Japanese Canadians ended when he was interned near Slocan. As a naturalised Canadian citizen, Tomey believed that the government did not have the right to imprison him simply because of his Japanese heritage. Tomey's son Keay remembers his father asking, "We're Canadians. How can they do this to us?"

❀

When the end of the Second World War was announced on the radio in August of 1945, Canadian soldiers returned home and families were reunited again. Yet life remained the same for the Japanese Canadians confined at the camps. It would be several years before they were permitted to return to the coast. Sadly, Tomekichi died on October 28, 1945 at the age of eighty while still interned at Slocan.

Tomekichi's children remember their mother often asking their father, "Why don't you tell the children about your family history?" Matsu wanted their children to know about Tomey's ancestry, his upbringing in Japan, and his role in building the Japanese immigrant community in Canada. Tomey simply replied, "When the lid of my coffin is closed, they'll all understand."

When families were evacuated to the internment camps, each adult was allowed 100 pounds of luggage; children were allowed 75 pounds. Families debated carefully about what to pack — kitchenware, bedding, and other necessities. *(JCNM photo, 1945)*

Road camp group portrait at Albreda, British Columbia, 1942. Tomekichi told his boys, "Take care, be safe, look after each other." *(Mas Yoshitake)*

Men from 18 to 45 years of age were sent to road camps. They were paid 25 cents per hour and worked 8 hours a day, 5 days a week, regardless of weather. In turn, the workers had to pay 75 cents a day for food and accommodation; their income was also taxed. Tomekichi's sons worked on the segment of the TransCanada Highway between Sicamous and Revelstoke. *(Misao Yoshitake, 1946)*

Many Japanese Canadians were housed in tents until the cabins were constructed.
(S. Inouye Fonds Inventory, ca. 1942)

These wooden cabins became the permanent homes of the Japanese Canadians interned in Slocan.
(Alec Eastwood Collection, 1942)

Japanese who did not have their Canadian citizenship, and those who protested the government policy of separating families, were sent to Ontario to a camp formerly used for holding German prisoners of war. Men who refused the order to leave their families to work at road camps, and those who disobeyed the dawn-to-dusk curfew were rounded up by authorities and imprisoned at this site. *(Joe Hayaru Oyama, 1942)*

Some Japanese were relocated to Alberta and Manitoba to work on sugar beet farms. This allowed family members to stay together. *(JCNM, 1943)*

60

Towards the end of the war, Japanese-Canadian families had to choose between relinquishing their Canadian citizenship and being deported to Japan, or remaining in Canada and relocating east of the Rocky Mountains. The Hommas decided to retain their Canadian citizenship. Several thousand Japanese Canadians left Canada before the Canadian government finally cancelled the deportations.
(JCNM, 1946)

61

Regrettably, while growing up Tomekichi's children never learned of their father's many contributions to the Japanese Canadian community. They gained a greater understanding of their father when they heard the eulogies delivered at his funeral. At Tomey's funeral, Mr. Iwaichi Kawajiri stood up and stated, "Although you (Homma) left this world without seeing any of your intentions bear fruit, there are many still remaining in Canada who will continue the fight. I don't know whether this will be possible during my lifetime, but I firmly believe your dreams will be realised. At that time, people will gather at your graveside and report it to you."

The Homma children remember how their father valued his Canadian citizenship. He instilled in his children the importance of learning English and of being a law-abiding citizen. Tomey sincerely believed that if he did these things, he would be a good Canadian.

Tomekichi's Buddhist funeral, Bay Farm outside of Slocan City, 1945. It was held in a school auditorium because a large number of people wanted to pay their respects.

(Homma family photo)

Nearly four years after Tomekichi's death, his third eldest son, Seiji, completed what his father began fifty years earlier. In March of 1949, Seiji Homma sat in the public gallery at the provincial legislature in Victoria, British Columbia. He witnessed the reading of the bill that granted the Japanese community the right to vote. Seiji wrote, "If only Dad could have been here with us to experience this victory. He would have been thrilled, as we were, by the jubilant news."

Although Matsu was not present at the legislature when the Japanese were given the right to vote, she expressed these words: "It's too bad Papa wasn't alive. It would have been an honour for him to witness this. Even though we're proud, Papa would have been prouder."

Throughout his life, Tomekichi Homma believed passionately in justice, dignity, and equality for all.

Family portrait taken at Tomekichi's funeral. The sign in Japanese posted to the right of the entrance to the home is a Buddhist custom stating there has been a death in the family. This was the first time in four years the Homma family had been reunited, as siblings were relocated in different internment camps. RCMP permission was required in order for them to travel to their father's funeral.
(Homma family photo, 1945)

His vision and leadership shaped and changed the emerging Japanese community in Canada. His contribution in the movement to achieve voting rights for Asians was a step towards making Canada a more democratic home for all.

THE VANCOUVER DAILY PROVINCE
A SOUTHAM NEWSPAPER

Published every day except Sunday and holidays at the southeast corner of Hastings and Cambie Street, Victory Square, in the City of Vancouver, Province of British Columbia by the Southam Company Limited.

VANCOUVER, B.C., WEDNESDAY, MARCH 9, 1949

They Have Earned Citizenship

A BILL was introduced in the British Columbia Legislature, this week, giving the franchise to reservation Indians and Canadian citizens of Japanese origin. The new legislation is in accord with the spirit of the times and, when adopted, will erase a blot from the British Columbia record.

It is entirely illogical that any citizen of Canada who is willing to accept the obligations and duties of citizenship should be denied any of citizenship's privileges, and voting is one of these. '

The granting of the franchise to Indians and Japanese will leave the Doukhobors the only racial group among us denied the right to the ballot. It is too bad that these must be regarded as lesser citizens, but the fault lies entirely with themselves. Whenever the Doukhobors show themselves ready to accept the obligations of citizenship, they will find the Legislature ready to remove their disability.

It will be necessary for us also to go a little further with our Japanese fellow-citizens. There is no use blinking the fact that these have been suffering from prejudice. The prejudice arose in the first place because the Japanese were in too great concentration on the Coast and it was strengthened by the war.

Now, the Japanese have purged themselves. They have accepted the principle of dispersal and have so conducted themselves in the interior of the province that they are not only accepted but are welcomed and admired.

It follows that the several disabilities under which they still labor should be removed. They should be accorded the same freedom of movement as other citizens. The old age pension bonus should be no longer denied them, and the bars which prohibit their entering certain professions should be removed. Some of these bars will vanish automatically with the winning of the franchise. The removal of others will have to be deliberate.

A bill was introduced in the provincial legislature to grant Japanese Canadians and First Nations the right to vote. This was a step towards achieving the privileges and rights that were universally enjoyed by other Canadian citizens.
(The Vancouver Daily Province, *March 1949*)

64

Postscript

Tomey's children, Yoshi Abe and Keay Homma, told the family stories that appear in this book. Other family members and close family friends also contributed their recollections.

At times, the Tomekichi Homma case has been presented in law schools in North America. It illustrates how the courts in the early twentieth century used legal deception to maintain discriminatory racial barriers.

Recently, Dr. Andrea Geiger, a historian and lawyer, researched and examined the case of Tomekichi's legal battle. She argues that British Columbia courts correctly applied existing law when they upheld Homma's challenge to the Provincial Voters Act, and that the Privy Council's decision was ill founded in its reliance on a phrase extracted from an 1863 American legal treatise.

Mr. Jinshiro Nakayama, a respected early Japanese immigrant, said the following of Tomekichi Homma:

> You have consistently sacrificed yourself for the public good. As for your great, distinguished service that contributed to the expansion of rights and interests of our compatriots, such service is unparalleled when compared to that of other small successful ones. "Canada's Homma" is the object of reverence by the Japanese communities overseas.

Tomekichi's descendants live in cities across Canada. There are five generations of the Homma clan. Two of Tomey's children are still living. His eldest daughter, Yoshi Abe, lives in Winnipeg,

Manitoba and his youngest son, Keay Homma, resides in Delta, British Columbia.

Tomekichi Homma's remains were returned to Vancouver, the city where his contributions to the Japanese community were most notable. He rests next to his wife, Matsu, at Mountain View Cemetery. Some of his cremated ashes were returned to Ichikawa City, Japan and placed in the ancestral Homma gravesite.

A school was built and named in his honour in Richmond, British Columbia. It is called the Tomekichi Homma Elementary School. In November 1991, Tomey's children and grandchildren proudly attended the opening ceremony of the school.

The few remaining possessions belonging to Tomekichi Homma are housed as an archival collection at the Japanese Canadian National Museum in Burnaby, British Columbia.

Copies of the books, *Canada no Hoko (Treasures of Canada)* and *Canada Doho Hatten Taikan Furoku (An Appendix to the Directory of the Development of Japanese Canadians)* can be found at the Japanese Canadian National Museum in Burnaby, British Columbia.

Tomekichi Homma Elementary School, Richmond, B.C. The school was officially opened in 1991. Hommas from across Canada attended the inaugural ceremony.
(Keay Homma, 1991)

Acknowledgements

The authors would like to thank the following individuals for the use of their family photographs.

ELIZABETH MAH
HAROLD AND KATHY STEVES
MITSUO YESAKI

Additional Photographic Contributors

JANET ABE
CITY OF RICHMOND ARCHIVES (CRA)
CITY OF VANCOUVER ARCHIVES (CVA)
IRVING HOUSE HISTORIC CENTRE MUSEUM (IHHCM)
JAPANESE CANADIAN NATIONAL MUSEUM (JCNM)
UNIVERSITY OF BRITISH COLUMBIA - SPECIAL COLLECTIONS
  (UBC-SC)
VANCOUVER PUBLIC LIBRARY (VPL)
WEST VANCOUVER ARCHIVES (WVA)

Special acknowledgement must be made to the National Association of Japanese Canadians for its financial support.

We wish to express sincere appreciation to the Japanese Canadian National Museum for its role in the publication of this book.

Other Notable Contributors

YOSHIMARU AND YOSHI ABE	DR. MIDGE AYUKAWA
LISA COLLINS	STANLEY FUKAWA
DR. ANDREA GEIGER	HASUE HOMMA
RON NISHIMURA	TIMOTHY SAVAGE
GRACE EIKO THOMSON	

We would like to recognize and thank David Hancock and the Hancock House staff who assisted in this project.

We are grateful for their dedication and commitment to publishing this story.

The authors would like to thank the many members of the Homma family for their participation in this project. Special mention must be made to Keay Homma for sharing his family stories. The Hommas value the opportunity to share the history of their patriarch, Tomekichi Homma.

The Authors

Tenney-Sean Homma and Carey Isaksson are educators in West Vancouver, British Columbia. They both have extensive experience working with elementary children. Their school district supports students from different cultures; ethnic diversity is celebrated and honoured.

Photos: www.urbanpictures.com

Bibliography

Abe, Y. 2003. "Tomekichi Homma." *Nikkei Images,* Spring, Vol. 8: 6–8.

Adachi, K. 1976. *The Enemy That Never Was: A History of Japanese Canadians.* Toronto ON: McClelland & Stewart Ltd.

Andie Barrie Show. 1988. Radio Station CFRB, Toronto, Ontario, Friday, September 23.

Ayukawa, M., Miki, R., & Shibata, Y. 2000. "Re-shaping Memory, Owning History Through the Lens of Japanese Canadian Redress." Catalogue celebrating the September 2000 opening of the National Museum of Japanese Canadians and Heritage Centre (now called the National Nikkei Museum and Heritage Centre), Burnaby, BC.

Curtis, Maureen. 1995. "WV Cannery Past Relived." *North Shore News,* December 13, pp. 17–18.

Geiger-Adams, A. 2002. "Excluding Suffrage from 'All Political Rights, Powers and Privileges' of Citizenship in Canada: The Privy Counsel's 1902 Decision in *Homma v. Cunningham.*" Unpublished manuscript, University of Washington at Seattle.

Geiger-Adams, A. 2003. "Pioneer Issei: Tomekichi Homma's Fight for the Franchise." *Nikkei Images,* Spring, Vol. 8: 1–5.

Hall, J.W. 1968. *Japan from Prehistory to Modern Times.* New York, NY: Dell Publishing Co.

Homma, K.T. 2003. "Personal Recollection of Tomekichi Homma." *Nikkei Images,* Spring, Vol. 8: 8–9.

Homma, T. 1977. "Looking Back by Tomekichi Homma." *The New Canadian,* August, pp.1–3

Ito, Roy. 1994. *Stories of My People, A Japanese Canadian Journal.* Hamilton, ON: Promark Printing.

The Japanese Canadians, A Dream of Riches. 1978. Vancouver, BC: Japanese Canadian Centennial Project.

Kadota, D., Kobayashi, C., Miki, R., & Schendlinger, M. 1988. *Justice in Our Time Redress for Japanese Canadians.* Vancouver, BC: National Association of Japanese Canadians.

Nakayama, J. 1940. *Kanada to Nihonjin (Canada and the Japanese).* Tokyo, Japan: Fuji Publishing Co.

Sansom, G.B. 1931. *Japan, a Short Cultural History.* Rutland, VT: Charles E. Tuttle Co.

Takata, T. 1983. *Nikkei Legacy: The Story of Japanese Canadian from Settlement to Today.* Toronto, ON: New Canada Publications.

Tanaka, Y. translated by Hashizume, W. 2000. "The Life of Tomekichi Homma." *Nikkei Voice,* February, p. 7.

Yesaki, M., Steves, H., & Steves, K. 1998. *Steveston Cannery Row: An Illustrated History.* Richmond, BC: Lulu Island Printing Ltd.

Yesaki, M. 2003. *Sutebusuton: A Japanese Village on the British Columbia Coast.* Vancouver, BC: Peninsula Publishing Co.

The first Homma Family Reunion was attended by many generations in Winnipeg, Manitoba. *(John Swan photo, 2003)*